WE PRESS

OURSELVES PLAINLY

NS

NIGHTBOAT BOOKS

CALLICOON, NEW YORK

La boue, nous l'avons bue, elle coulait entre nos lèvres; jusqu'à ce que nous ne sentions plus rien de la soif. Nous nous sommes réveillés, le soir; nous pouvions bouger et marcher à nouveau. Tu as usé alors tes dernières forces à taper du poing sur mon visage, ma poitrine, en me reprochant ta soif, et d'avoir bu cela.

BERNARD-MARIE KOLTÈS

On ne meurt pas seul, on se fait tuer, par routine, par impossibilité, suivant leur inspiration. Si tout le temps j'ai parlé de meurtre, quelquefois à demi camouflé, c'est à cause de cela, cette façon de tuer.

DANIELLE COLLOBERT

Everyone carries a room about inside him.

FRANZ KAFKA

WE   PRESS

OURSELVES PLAINLY

I will go then... No need to convince me in this direction... Nor for that matter to dissuade me... My mind is made... The door there and beyond the door... The thing instead... Instead of which other thing... To put a word on it... The desire exists... In the skin of the thing the word detached from the thing... It is not so important to make proofs of this... The wood of the door... The sound of the door closing... Wood against wood... It is a pleasure to hear... To receive the sound into the body... It is its own skin... With its own words detaching... I would like for the cessation of these words... For the cessation of this lurch in their direction... It is so absolute... I would like to abolish it... This... This drive or passion... The promise of that particular pleasure...

Withheld… Only because of the positioning… If I could just turn to face this way instead… But the whole of it follows… It is indescribably painful… This one movement… It multiplies itself into the mouth and into the hands… I see here the marks left by the movement… They replicate themselves into the many things such that they are unidentifiable with themselves… I don't quite see them… It is not a mysticism… Certainly not… The age is rife with mysticisms and this is a misfortune… It obfuscates… If only to press ourselves plainly… The mystic is leaned all the while against a plate of glass… The glass conveys the heat of the sun and the light of the sky but all sensory experiences are mitigated by the glass… Other than the press of the body against the glass… It is for the senses that we do this... That we stand on one side or other of the glass... Sometimes the glass breaks... We break it... We do this deliberately... We lean too heavily or else throw something directly... I can allow for this... The impulse turns to compulsion... We feed like farm animals from a poisoned trough... We do this... We speak of doing this languorously... I accept the freedoms... The doors that close and open... The bodies that fall unheld into the next day... I would like to kiss you... The field of vision narrows with the century... We stand on one side or other of the century and it is the same century... It folds us in... We come out of this war just as we enter into it... I go to great lengths to remember it... It escapes... No point telling it to me... It is just outside the window... I cross the street and I am crossing the moors... It is very effective... I mean the disjuncture... I could be anywhere... Adoring... I have not pardoned... This war pulls at all the other wars... The strands of wars... I hold myself up just as you do... The centuries... The emaciations... The maps make us skinny... The blue veined rivers swallowed into the yellowing paper... The tears at the creases folded over and over... The names made illegible... I should like for my own name made illegible... For its trace to be adjacent but undisclosed simply to the blue vein of the river... The marks pulsate... This is as they make themselves known to me... In the way they have of trembling... It is not electrical...

It is not thick either in the way that throbbing is... Fragile... A tremor... Simplified in the grain of wood... In the skin... The sensation... You turn away... I am not mad... Not as you would have it... I have sorrow that has marked me up... From the bottom I walk up to Berry Head... The winds here are delirious... The grasses lie flat... And the waters rush at the rock... I lose the sad part of me... I lose it against the ground... The wind picks it up and pushes it at me... I choke crying out and then it is gone... Dried up... And the little word detaching... A history of disappearances... I love each of them... I cup a small flame into my hands and blow on it gently... A whole wood catches fire with the flame... A blue light fills full the sky... And the names rain ash onto

a ground... I catch them like snowflakes...
Each one is unique and they all taste the
same... Of the same death... I want to say that
the collection begins small but it is big at the
start... Bigger than I can fathom... In the
museum of art all of the bodies are naked...
They are at various stages of decomposition...
I touch each one nonetheless... I blow on some
of them... The dust settles around the dry
bones... I roll in the dust... The museum is
dispassionate and wears me down... Between
each room is a door of glass to push through...
I scratch at the glass... A letter sent out of
the desert does not arrive... A fugitive traces
the whole length of a shoreline... There is the
one who waits and the one who makes an
offering... When I come down from the hill I

leave the cormorants on an outcrop of rock... It is winter in that country as in no other... The walking man collects small fragments into his hands... He divulges none of what he finds... He takes it simply... I walk beside but already it is the ghost of the man who accompanies me... He would want for the moment to be behind him... To be alone with the remembrance that he fills into himself... Full... He makes of the present a fleeting thing... An adoration... The distinction between inside and out... The doors into the casbah open sideways so that it is not possible to see in from the street... I imagine them palatial... Labyrinthine... It is only an imagining... The rooftops press the sky into itself... It hooks into the smoke stacks...

I think of this unseen architecture... The upward moment in building... Its concealment... The left eye muddies and distorts... A dark ring becomes visible at the navel... The disease hardens the underside... I go there... The first days there is a mad hope... A series of small explosions... They begin in an interior... The light is low and the organs stiffen into the littlest of stones... The fragility makes it even more beautiful... The mouth-blown glass burst into blue particles... A charge of infidelities... I will go then... The sound rises from the floorboards... Horse hair drawn over a taut string... The strain of it... Pulling sound from a wooden throat... The windows of an entire village have been boarded up... And the houses wrapped in plastic sheeting... I walk through the village and draw the sky close for covering... We recoil from that absence... The heaving of the bruised earth underfoot... The taverns are nonetheless full of brawling men... I don't sleep until morning... It is safest then... Away from the rush of blood to the temples... Hindemith or Rachmaninov... What is the name of the young woman inside the prison wall... The garden is not now planted... The swamp is motioning... The deaths we hope for... We starve the wanting parts... A conviction... The destitute parts... Withhold them... What is the song... A season closed against the body of a dog... What will I roam... The starved and wanting parts... The relinquished utterances... Who spoke them...

That the pleasures wear us through… Do you go to Paris often… It is simple mimicry… The platitudes… Stepping onto the platform is the simplest action to accomplish… But remaining… You stare at me so… The same gift is promised… What will become of the bodies… I have broken with everything… These few things… A turquoise stone from Morocco… A silver ring from Afghanistan… A threadbare rug… My sister wishes me well… The time of the religions is passed… A belief of any kind… The brothers beat the sisters… The mothers the sons… At the border the guard asks to see the papers… In the new world the body is listed under additional comments… And their issuance… I receive the permission… What do you imagine it to be... The bone broken into two distinct pieces... A fracture more complete... A limb positioned singly... I make the argument for the daughters... I draw the city names from a hat... From this I determine the trajectory... We wait for... At a roadside... Gravel... What is the sentence for behaving... We slept in a single bed... Now there are too many praises... There is evidence of it in the gait of young libertines... And the lean of new buildings... The lovers all turn eventually to despotism... In the field guide of reminiscences I find a passage devoted solely to devotions... The blue light of dusk fallen against an exposed flank... The writhing of obsolescence... The turbulent yearning of wheat fields and herons stooped over marshlands... The young who cut lines into their hearts... The chafings... The bulwarks... The seething... The history is the same belief in shipyards and fellatio... It is all stuttered into me... And the reason for it is in the disbelief... What it will be when the bodies sicken... I cannot now... The symptoms are expertly manipulated... I touch but what cannot be touched... The steam rises off the tarmac at an early hour of the morning... I know morning by the sickness in the body... The moaning that catches me... Why must you... There are seven unarmed cities... The first is abandoned... The second is mute... The third is forgotten... The rest are a fantasy... I have been to each and carry nothing of them with me... Coordinates are devised for such things... And sequences of numbers... Platelet counts... Spurned divinities... The mouth mimics a threshold... We speak from that oversight... The compressed places turned further inward... In the night there is howling and in the day it continues unabated... The disturbances are overthrown... And the waters are engorged from so many bodies... I would like now to be proven wrong... I follow the hoof prints of the wild ponies in the tangle of gorse in December... What is the distance from here to the door... From here to any one place... There is a shudder in the walls that becomes breathing... Is it clay or sandstone... You would rather it undisclosed... Torn into the skin but sewn up immediately and overgrown... Without a reference... The

constituent parts of a rooftop are seductive...
The chimney or tar paper... The parapet...
The water tower or tile... Eaves...
Weathervane... The parameters that mark off
the space between the rail line and nothing...
Adrift... The separations are illusory and
walkable... Who will fly and who will get up...
That the lover reminded me of the sea... That
the missing language became the first reason
to go missing... That the body disappeared
into the mark it made for itself... That
the battering did not wake me from sleep but
went on battering... That the singularity was
theologically unsound... And the whirring
wearing... That the text said broken without
accusation... The shattered parts found and
assembled... It isn't constant... What you

make of madness the scattering… I have no fear of what is unbound but binding… The gauze strips hang loosely from the torn frame… Yellowing… The body lurches away from its place… What is the thing that you always say… No point repeating it… I have the text here somewhere… In a pocket or woven into the inside of my shirt… It is easily summarised… The way is divided… The letter goes unwritten… The train does not leave the station… The street darkens… She sleeps uncovered… The river widens… The man comes… The lover is impotent and unadorned… We are naked for the moment… I grant you this one torment… The authorities sexed them and they died… I was the fornicant… You were apprised… Love… It was nothing... The thing fingers me... It is not simply the inconstancy... The steps are numbered not counted... All nine or twelve of them... And they are as long as years... I quicken... It stays stuck to me... In the desert I imagine it peeled back... A whole length of it... Stripped of its permeability... The promise of sense is made... I reject it... It rejects me first... I could never stand the woodwinds... The strings made it tolerable... There is blood in the stool in the snout... The lungs are perforated... I stroke it back... The distance is unalterable... I count it out... The outpouring... Theories of synchronism are written down... In the library the waking guard pulls the patrons from sleep... Shake shake... Shake shake... Sweeps the sleeping readers onto the street... Eddying... For the sake of simplicity the wars become one war... And it is decried... No one leaves the houses... The streets become empty and it is a metaphor for their undecidedness... It prompts moments of inability... The silence not of forgetting... The massacres the mediocrity... We stand each on one side or other... The burn the bruise... I overlook the boundary... We stand each on one side or other of the crossing line... From navel to groin and upwards... What will it who will it... The thing bursts out of me... Closed or open... I kiss you anyway... The stinking whole of it... Pressed into the sagging planks of wood... A margin as granular... Incremental... It is undone from the pillar the field the... Not in strips but dust...

Unconstituted and misremembered... Now the body is bone hooking skin... Not even this... You insist that it is otherwise... I could walk from here to Donostia... I imagine the other side and it is the very same side... I look through it to you... Or else through you to the part that isn't waiting... That doesn't wait... The swell of the lover ocean... I remark the difference... I shift my weight onto the other foot... I kneel or stand... It is worse and worse... In the night unsleeping... What the mouth makes of horror... The people gather in the public square for the concentration... A period of time spent in silence for the moment that is gone... And taken with it... A concentration... I go there and I am quiet... In the spent parts it is gathered there... Folded onto the time before... What manhood do you aspire to... A wild hunger... A sadistic undertaking... The whole of it... These are the last days... I manage just fine just fine... The long last... It goes empty... There are the deaths that are unaccounted for... I don't put anything away... The disorder of fields and machineries... Impressed... It detaches just the same... The madnesses bound to a common circuitry come apart from one another in the way that a constellation might redesign itself... A derangement... It need not be neurological... Nor even bacterial... In the closed room there is talk of a new virus sucked into the old body... I feel none of it... This particular thesis was a defence of the palpable... The claim to a body or a language... Of trust... Or immobility... A carcinogen interrupts... I make it up as I go... The field of chamomile... Imagine it... A perversion of the hemispheres... What we might make of it... In simple misshapen terms... Globular or crystalline... We speak of an immediacy at the borders... The suppression of place names and some woven fabrics... Great swaths of vegetable-dyed cloth overlain with small pinpricks of blood and pomegranate beads... At another time we might eat together... I say this... What do you expect for it... Did we live here for a time... Did we do these things... I distrusted it... If the manual of style had performed otherwise... I made a life for myself of soliloquy... If I face this way instead there is the beach imported from another place... My sister walks there and eats berries dropping seeds for the birds in winter... If the magnitude... I can't really say... But that the door opens awkwardly... The walls fell outward and she was left with only the sky for ground... The barbarism... The indecency she said... And it was not... In looking up at nothing... The phrase I cannot go on... But that I can and I do... What detaches is embedded... We pull at it and drive the scar from the skin... Myself that I killed kill... The whole time watching... Killed it... I saw into the eyes... Now it is after... There is no record of what was said... Nor the transition from seeing to being seen... Listless... I move closer... In retreat... You advance a meaning for the hunger that doesn't... Can't... I feed

on it… Eat what is rotten and leave the rest…
You become foreign to me… For this I reject
you… The threat of nostalgia is immediately
corrected… It is a week now and the sun is
low in the sky… The same end to every day
and it is unforgiving… What comes out of me
is a boundless rage… Nothing is as it should
be… There is the one who waits and the one
who denies… You are wrong to pity me…
You were indiscriminate even then… Pushing
at the soft vulnerable parts… Imprinting what
you were willing to bestow… You were both
conciliatory and demanding… The history
wears itself in… On my knees the light streams
down toward me… It has all of the qualities of
water save one… You want to know which
one… The difference between say a tire track

and a fire mark… Bruise foraged from burn…
The suggestion of the immediacy is transported
to the present across whatever distance… A
compression layered of other moments just
like it… Incrusted… In the remaining scar for
example or discoloration is the laceration or
impact and whatever exuded sealed over
peeled back and distorted… A cry perhaps or
breath withheld… In the glass pane is the
accumulated shadow of all who pushed past it
and across a particular threshold… We wipe it
back… All that we seek is refusal… The details
are unremarkable… When I walk to the tip of
Hope's Nose… It is the same suicide… What
trails after… A frightful silence is followed by
a frightful noise… There is no hurry now…
There is only the time from before… We stand

each on one side or other of a desire and it is the same desire... We manage the foreground... All the time composing... Speaking a line broken into lies... The difference might be negligible... It begins an ache... Does it warrant acknowledgement... The culture is unsympathetic... The bone breaks in three places... And the heart... Is it for the brokenness... The whole of it gathered into the shrapnelled parts... The cells belie the incidence... She comes running... Again and again she comes running... The threshold is each time replaced... We wait for... It warns... Who minded it... We steal the message line for line... The disease is parasitic... We welcome... The distance too is negligible... What I tell you... Gathered at the corners of

things... The invisible lacerating particulate...
I take a deep breath... The canvas towers
over... It is leaden and inarticulate... The
small individual rooms fasten each to the
other... The shadows crowded at the
doorways... Passageways... Clusters of them
fastened in infinite combinations... Each room
to another... Deepening a course... We fail
at... The bodies shoved like this... Grossly
over-estimated... Thinning against the sides...
Almost invisibly... Indivisibly... Look at them
all... An industrious... The foghorn sounds
now... I burrow into the floorboards with the
small animals... There was no mystery but
relegation... The doors began closed before
they opened... We walk this far... Have you
been to... I must have slept right through... It

was there in the residual buildings... Entered a city through its gates... It was unnamed and disappearing... The schools were enviably quiet... All the shrieking sucked into the visible dust... There was one country in particular... It became the particularity of every country... The shamed overlay of faces... Even the small corner of grass... What grows there... From the bottom up... I dig it out of the ground... It and all the others... What it makes of the dust... The ideal is disproportionate... The edifices are made in contempt of the bodies... I stand in the stalls... Each of them... It is not possible... The ignorance in constancy... Not one... The worldliness of geographies... With a brush to scrub the surfaces raw... I grieved grieving...

Parcelled out the small formations into smaller ones... Tiny little disasters... Handled carefully and placed gingerly onto small metal trays... Then labelled... We make these manifestations into ourselves... What happens when... Shorn and emaciated... I forget all of it... The disordered remembrances... There is knocking... It comes from inside... A strangulation... The tripes pulled up into the ribcage... A thick elastic band... Not breathing... Heat in the skin of the face... The faces... Hands flipped back... A plasticity... It was touching... A hardness... Twist of a straight bone... Close to snapping... It releases... Leveraged... What do you suppose... Does she mark time anymore... There is no sense... In the end the... It doesn't matter that... For once... After lifting all those days up off the ground and carrying them to the far corner of a garden... Any garden... Was once a garden... The boards tied up with loose wire... I catch on it... The dug up parts... And the birds brought here in winter... I wanted... The weight added to my own weight... It diminished me... Sprawling... The small hips splayed... Pelvis hitting the concrete... Again lifted... I wipe it all over me... The blood the snot the... Evacuations... Whole neighbourhoods... The small birds in cages... It doesn't matter that they sing... Who invented this belief in song... What mattered were the ground up remnants of bones... Who claimed them... Set them out or stole them... Sold them... If for no reason... I dropped it...

And scorn... It is over now... I say this... In the winter months there are three hours of light... I counted the minutes from the ziggurats to the Broad... The Fens strangled between tall posts and broad animals... The footpath turns on itself... Leading out and in simultaneously... Flattening a surface of sight... If it were considered from the underside... Even the river stilled... The many thinkers made a fuss of the language... We misunderstood all of it... Not the least of which... The road ends where I leave it... At the edge of itself... If only the walking were directed... The projection declared a form of disappearance... It manifested a sharpness... Of colour... Or light... A transparency grafted over a thick darkness... I look through it to the hard immovable... It is a way of watching for the next thing... It doesn't come... The next thing is always behind me... Founded on the desire for the next thing... It doesn't exist... Outside of the desire... An overlay of hands... Or something... Built up... And extinguished... A thing placed between... It needn't necessarily be glass... Nor even breath... A membrane or skin... What I mean by... I cried out... It is a solipsism to try to articulate any of this... To reason it into a measure of being... The books burn as they are written... Who wanted... Was wanted... It happened that the sea rose higher that year... The marsh edged nearer... I walk a great distance... You underestimate... I never desired what was familiar... Nor asked for...

It isn't the first time... Mornings the light grows dim... It settles into me... For a time it is bearable... It becomes indistinguishable... The marsh from the bedrock... Erosion from speaking... It doesn't matter that we are mute... That the still moment is passed... That the shriek is swallowed down... The break leaves no visible mark... The hand grabs at what is missing... But every other thing in its place... The matt of scar tissue or sediment... There are blockages... The passageways... It is not a barrenness... But burden... I start... Startle you... The illness is indescribable... It slowed the whole of everything... The lifting the swallowing... I entered... The foreground repositioned... I touched it... One after another the questions came at me... I fled and

was scolded... The wars are indistinguishable... I carry it in my arms... The distance
fluctuates... I walk from one end to another of
a city... I cannot cross this room... I carry it
out... Many times over... That noise... The
wood swells against the frame... It makes an
enclosure... I turn inside... There were more
than could be accounted for... They were
listed... Followed by many blank pages for
those who would come after... They didn't...
The history was a culmination... We were
despondent... Blaming... The thing moved
into itself... And into the rest of us... There
was no sourcebook... Only a yearning...
Complaints... And admonishments... We
bowed our heads... It wasn't true... The doors
flung open... Broken off the door posts...

What lit that particular sky... It isn't good to describe it... It is buried now... The thing and what preceded it... I manage a small distance every day now... It sickens me... I don't wish for... The ruined parts provide comfort... I pull myself to the edge... I will go then... It was nothing that couldn't have been avoided... The fixtures were torn from the cavities... Gaping... The house hunched... Wounded... The architects argued for scrap and the archaeologists said what remained... It was new again... I shudder to think... It comes to this... I go without... I go there without you... What is left... It rendered speechless... The whole language dispersed... Feathers among the wood chips... Dust by the side wall... The beleaguered part of me whimpered... I saw it… For the last time saw it… An imperceptible tremor and it entered me… So slightly… A seduction… Dead and thereafter… I vomit and heave… A stain by the window where water entered… There is the one who wants and the one who is pardoned… Each law a violation… I don't read now… It fixes and confuses… I object to the organising principle… The mishap of approximation… An idea of wholeness in the place of what is broken… Is it so easy… Step down or reach over… I cannot now leave or complete… I crane my neck to see past the pigeons to beaten… I will finish this and then stop… The opening narrows… It is for none of us… What the speaker said he meant… I admit defeat… A meaning is made for this… It is repudiated

with the same breath that causes it to happen...
I grow away... Stop speaking... Just for a
time... I scarcely know now... What takes
hold is a fear and a belief attached to the fear...
The voice that comes out of the throat hard...
I whisper it and it vanishes... It mightn't have
been so... A cry opens in a closed space... The
fortressed language uninhabited... There is no
possibility of entry... The passage the
impasse... This corner where I stand... The
accumulated efforts to place me here... I think
because of it... The thinking gets me nowhere...
The brilliancy proclaimed... I might have
spoken otherwise... The edifices risen in the
way of the words that manufacture... Built of
the same materials... This idea of infallibility...
I look closely at the weakened crossbeam...

The ardent architecture... The cold steel and it bends... Dwarfs the rest of the city... The people there looking up... Proportionally... The scale the measure is its own religiosity... The disciples of this new form of building... The birds cascade broken necked into the urban graves... Unadorned... Unadoring... We walk beneath... It turns out in the same way... I turn in... The sound stops now... Listen for it... The wood burnt or damaged... The bow frays... It's as the body... I want for you... Hoarse... The remaining sounds driven underfoot... Forced into the grain with the smaller unnamed particles... They smother there with the small animals... Even the unwalled city... I walk through it... A whole winter of walking... Unboundaried... The

thing that lay beyond... There was nothing
there... Many times I sought it out... In the
same place and in other places... I pushed pass
the doors again and again to where the doors
disappeared altogether... Unhooked from
their posts... Unbuilt but suggested... A sound
pushed back into the throat... Collected
there... Accreting... Pestilent... A carrier... It
catches in the very air... I breathe it... You
breathe it... It spits up its own strain of
madness... If you will believe... Just this...
The fact of a singular strain... Drawn through
many many bodies... Attaching each to one...
The same strain repeated... Nauseatingly...
Pulled from the surface to a depth... It
excruciates... Listen... There are blueprints...
Drawings and designs... Many times over...

Layers and layers of lines facing in all directions... Indicating... Barring and traversing... It is not so readable now... Now that the buildings have fallen... A half death it is said... But who is saying... I take it into me... It falls further... The fall is calculated... A mass of... Or rubble... I peer into it... Even the distance is manufactured... I see less and less of it... It loses a surface... I walk over it unknowing... It is with me now... The first days it is visible... There are pardons... Abject... I balk at... The present is fussed about... Smoothed over with premonitions... I find the hook lodged in a throat... Pull... I turn inside... Release... Irreversibly... All that follows... At Berry Head I wish for nothing... The seeds of wild grasses... The frittered edge... It falls from there... Overlooking... What waters... What rock... The scribbled limestone... The voices proliferate toward a benediction... A small metal spoon scoops the hearts out... What feral... What civilised... I have no need for... Seizes upon... The last city is not a city at all... The absences obliviate... Unspeaking... I stop... The cut glass at the throat... Eviscerating... Hollows out what is left... Leaves nothing... I go there without you... Massing then bursting... A small over-burdened liver... A mangled spleen... We bear... Bury... Heart spilling blood into the weakened parts... Vomit it into me... How many times leave... Abbreviated and monstrous... For the time bereft... And swollen... Lumped grievously together... The skin weakens there... Striated and torn... It spreads indiscriminately to the other parts... I go there anyway... By train for the signals... The sideways motion emptied of itself... What it is that holds me up... There is a last time and it is unspeakable... Held by indisputable strands to every other thing... I lean this way and can feel it... A whole body maladjusts... The new cities are gated... The usual questions unasked... We are turned away... Turn away... I head back... I am as tall as the thatch roof but the little road widens to let the cars pass... These are demonstrations... The raised track denies an up looking... The people look down at their gods... Who made the monotheism... Wanted... What wanted... I sample the offerings... Rose coloured or drawn... The deities masturbate... I encounter Chernobyl in the body of a girl... A far-off place... Fancy wanting that... The split cell... A devotion... Such strange light... A grey mottled wall... Castilian... It throttles the ground... I walk only the shorter distances... The breadth of my arms pushing at barriers... Reach for the floor... Then crawl... I am small as need be... Unforeseen... And punishable... How close... Even so I am cold... Many times say... A confused surface... Stupefied... What loses me... I die of it... House worn... It is overdue now... I imagine an affection... It could simplify... But we don't find it... First large and then small... The shape of it known... And forlorn... It magnifies the insistence...

Here in the corner farthest from the door... A faint cry and it grows... Every other thing silenced... I pick up and replace... The room tips in the direction of an other thing... I catch on it... Ridicule... She stands still in a wide open... Cavernous... Hail on a rooftop... Drought at her knees... She doesn't kneel or protest... A garden in its entirety... Planted in her mouth... She wears dirt into the palm... Shoves grasses into the docks... Severs the living from the breathing parts... Dear sweet myopia... Pulses... In the midst of the sentence... The senses are desperate... I will go then... There is a last thing... And none of it... I say for the sake of the echo... Hammering... A quiet blast over a lake... A lit sky and writhing... Asphyxiate... You demand of me... It doesn't reach... Habitually I am famished... So I will eat some before... I kiss you... It comes at me... I wretch and am silent... Silence... If it dies in sleep... If it dies choking... If it dies rent... If it spills blood... If I should... I lie down in it... Only the blue flowers grow... In the closed space... In the privacy of my own pain... A remnant and worn... I kiss it instead... I part... Pull it open... Misuse it... The manner of a moment... Dislodging... It needn't stick like that... The imperceptible violations... We wait for... And want... I demanded continuance... The burst vessels gorge at the throat... A flourish and I reach for it... Senseless... I roll in it... I press into the floor which is no different than the body... A suffusion... I declare all of it... And

then I am silent... There is so much... If it... I
lie down anyway... Who is she... There is an
uncertainty in the body... A grievance against
a thing that is unimagined... And so rejected...
It radiates a kind of heat... I move over and
think nothing of it... I might speak... I am
alone... In a lavatory someone beseeches me...
I tempt... Am tempted... I remark on a
shooting range... There are two of us... It
eradicates... Not just the river... The
plurality... It quiets... Is quiet... What were
we... The house becomes visible at a corner...
There is a pain now that is not the same pain
and it belittles me... And this grief here coiled
into my hip... I am ill equipped... If you must
die then die before morning... If you must live
then live on... Through the glass there is a

bone structure and it is wrapped in swaths of light... It loosens from me the sensorial parts... They are ingrained and underfoot... If I were to give them a language they would detach just as I do... There is a thought structure too and it is rupturing... It comes apart in my hands and I wipe them along the baseboards where the light catches just as visibly... The waters rise... The village crouches and chokes... If you must leave then leave now... A divided sky and I marvel at it... It is the same space newly gridded... We stand each on one side or other of a conjecture and it is hardening... I stand apart from it... Disquieted... The falsehood of the glass house the topiary... Smoke curls out of the bodies... I look at all of it and I wretch just the same... The symphonies grate on me... Their grandeur... Their baseness... I look and then look away... The force is in the swinging gate... A paper book and it obviates... I smell it strongly... You deny the deaths and my inability... My organs slide out of me... You steady yourself and the wall... A window and it is shattering... I catch them in one hand... I manage just fine... The downhill and I see my way to it... It is late now and so impossible... There is the one who wants and the one who falls behind... We take pleasure there... It kisses my mouth... I sing with it... Singe... There is desolation... And indiscreet... It is a nakedness in language... A dissolution... In the event that it should disappear... That it should be capitulative... There is a banner for such things... Transparent or torn... A textile nailed to a stick and trembling... We stand each on one side or other of a violence and it is the same violence... In the mouth... The mouth foremost... I make a signature of it... A fount of praises and they are immaculate... Immaculate and catastrophic... It is another way of being dirty... In the earthward stretch of the unnamed paradises... Sexed and already bestial... Found and unfounded... A dearth of place names and indiscretions... We are unsurpassed... The moment precedes us and we stalk what is left of it... In remembrance... In facility... It exceeds us and itself... You follow me and have none of it... A gesture for the door and the futility... What part of what is left and I discard it... In the city centre there is a peril and it enters through the doorway unaccompanied... An adoration and it offers me... I stuff the cracks full of it... For the sound as it surfaces... Querulous... Divided... The scandal is in the acquiescence... That the writer should have written and made postures instead... That the institution sought its vocation in mediocrity... That the offerings were already decided... The spackled walls fold outward for the living and the pitied... I walk it over and undecided... I pull at the door handles and mark up the woodwork... Scratch at it... Finely... The incisions... Indescribable... It doesn't bleed... The hard parts harden and the skin thickens... Do you claim it... Instead of... The simultaneous degradation of stalwart and fruition... Needless to say... I cross the street and it is the same street and it bends into the house and out through the body... The same body and it compresses... The sameness of grieving... Fingerfuls... Bedded and raving... You stand there... Standing or lying down a pressure reserved for the clavicle... At the closed throat... Instead of what other thing... It is fantastical and hated... You for example... It was nothing approaching prodigal... Not the return nor the son... And he was screaming... And screams on... Who raises a fist... Who pisses along his leg... I lick it in and I swallow... The overture is funereal... Bombast at the fissure... And faint... There is the one who watches and the one who worsens... A cloth map unfolded and it makes the decision... I touch the faint parts and the eroded edge of rock... In deciding between seaward and a tea parlour... It wants all... And the widowed screeching mammals with their inconvenienced demeanour... A pain comes and it is greater than every other pain... It doesn't stop being cold... I make light of it... In the corner there is a rucksack... I rifle through the contents... Paper and keys... They may be mine or someone else's... I fold it back... And enter discreetly... In the metal hinge or happenstance... The lock rummaged for finding... Open and open... I look inside and it deepens... There is a fallout shelter in my memory... But I am not thinking of this... Not even the body as it is laid out or pressed upon... Its mutterings and they are faint or else fantasies... Does it matter... Matter the monster or these findings... I end up at unease... It is as severe as the other time... Queasy and disaffected... What was it about the last time... Was it quintessential... The body redirected or squandered... The door there and beyond the door... The distance between language that is spoken and language that is written... Mediating the throat in relation to the mouth and the lungs... An inhalation and it is too sudden and so breaking... Neck bent at a corner of floor and wall... The smell of an aberration and it is transparent... It means to be hospitable... Creased and worn... Permeable... But for the vacancy... I enter or I exit... The memory persists... It is not the same memory nor even approachable... An adoration... It tugs at the

straps... Unties face from fact... It murmurs
and makes itself abstract... A riverbed
indistinguishable from an edge and I walk
there... Imagine walking there... The instant
is pardoned for overreaching itself... There
are landslides... The walking man goes on
walking... Someone lags behind... The steel
doors are the weight of several bodies at
once... They push in... Scuff the floor... What
is institutional or tolerable... The fires set off
the revolutionaries... They each demanded
something... You watch as it happens... In
your tall way of watching... Looking down...
I catch what falls from you... In the way of
residue or excess... Pulling... You want and
deny... A broad horse and a sunken marsh...
Was it a familiarity... A movement... Small

parcels of the habitual dolled out... The little savageries and we delight in them... These things called delicacies... Under the red tiled roof the bed gouged and forgotten... Recited... Alphabetical... This might be uphill... I cross the heath and never... It didn't matter that it was real or invented... The language of it persists... In the whittled Giacomettis... Do you waste what... It might be simpler than... For example breathing... The eye trained upward... Pulling at the taut line of sight... Toppling fixtures and fledgling... There were democracies and there was running water... It was not warranted but ingrained... What miseries... What pharmaceuticals... The cities were privy to all of it and made instances of complaint and astonishment... There was a

conversion and it was made irregular... A
currency and it was exceptional... There were
no distinctions... Only a graduated incline and
it led nowhere else... I was there... I watched
as it came apart... In a mouth and overhead...
Unheard of... The grandsons rape the
daughters... The brothers the nieces... It
culminates in the soft spot... The skin lit up
from inside... And it is derided... There are
the irritations and you notice them... A train
ride and it is demented... I lie on the top
bunk... Inches from the ceiling... The stout
man yells obscenities when I move to the
floor... Smoke without stacks and rundown
mountains... A distance of rubble and scrub...
I go back and forth in each direction not
sleeping... What do you think of... You grant

me this one impatience... Your finger rubs a wooden rut... There is the framework and there is the catch... I run for it... You close the door behind me... We stand each on one side or other of the door and it is the same door... It is the same voice scoffing... It might have been fantastic... I lurch toward a shape... It is the same sickness and it mounts me... I make amends and it is later than anticipated... At the threshold there is screaming and a disappointment... I stroke it back... You hand it to me... Creaturely and attributed... For the moment... I take a step and it is pardoned... We do not meet... I make carvings out of the atrocity and set it on the window sill... It is not so much a reminder as a wistfulness and it is in the passing bodies... The fortunes are made with and without the images... We recant nonetheless... For the castrato who is not limping... And the rest of us who resign over it... It is altogether objectionable... The score is misremembered and attempted... The fountain is deep as the hips and waterless... I enter first and you follow... I touch the concrete bottom... There is weeping and no adjustment is made for the awkwardness... A sky and it is lit with heaving... First my own and then yours... I kick at it... There is nothing but the slow city and it offers release and a skin... Which is it... I take each choice into my mouth and don't swallow... The strings are enervated and the boards shiver... You stand over and interrupt... Why must you... The fragility is mine to begin with... There is moaning and a hand... I move over a drenched surface and tighten... There is a hardness and it weakens... I break into the seamlessness... Why can't you... For this time naked... No one startles... I am watchful and for the time I close... And then closer... It crosses and then crosses over... First the rivers then the sentiment... The bridge bears its weight of phenomena... I walk out... It is colossal and forbidden... It begs before beginning... I put it there... I was the stranger one... It comes back... There is the one who warns and the one who disappears... The desert as I imagine it... Desire as I desire it... It can only ever begin... The room wider and then shrunken... I huddle in a corner... Sprawl across the doorstop... There is talk of a settlement...

Nobody inhabited... There is a system and there are its contrivances... It could be any of us... Who is the first to wonder... I make accounts of it... In the thirties the membranes loosen then tear... There is no affinity... Only suspicion... What leaks out and then some... A series of small droplets tabulated into numerical values... From the room from the window and still... Counted out and then repeated... I refuse nothing... Not even the gloating... They arrive unattended... One and then the other... Each time the same... There is a balcony and an imagining... I catch it with one hand and conceal it with another... The protectorate forbade speaking... In the first instance the symptoms were of no interest... The bodies agglutinating into a light... They revelled in the pleasantries and took their clothes off... The country doctor laid the horses bare... It was remarked upon then settled... The sequences were misremembered... Foremost then most of all... In the afternoon the light dimmed and the prospects for reconciliation vanished... There is the one who says nothing... It it this one that I follow... Across the mud and gorse into dusk... When the rain comes I huddle in closer... Wrap a scarf over a mouth... In the manner of the blue octavo notebooks... The rooms meticulously folded away from one another... It sinks in... Marsh up to the knees and hands clawing to get in... Whatever it was you saw... I anticipate none of it... Board or burrow... It is the same desire... The same fright... For once there is food to be eaten... The years add up to the same thing... The creatures are sickly... I roll in it with them... You kiss it at the same time... An improbable lover... Laid over at Sofia on the way to Heathrow... Were you ravenous then... The English bought up the mountainsides and the rains washed the roads into the river... I saw it all from the window... The tapered towers... Small children mendicating pieces of history... The public square swung right knocking the bells from the towers and the cities shifted onto their behinds... It won't do someone said... But it did all right... A line of small perforations... They are perfect and unseemly... I enter the tunnel and the walls fall in... The drowned face up in the shallowest parts... There are rivulets and a small stream of light... Wan as the faces peering out... It is not warranted but profitable... So you say... We struggle for a time... There are whimpers and cries... In the last hours the refugees are turned out... Light passes through them in the way that hunger does... The religions die with them... It needs saying at least one more time... For the sake of the horse at Hermagor and for the horse at Turin... And for the horse in the corridor... What is barbaric is a commonplace... I go there... The map lays out what is bearable... The rest is thrust upon the unwitting bodies... A leap or lurch... Either way it is distasteful... She comes running... Again and again she comes running... The sound is torn from a mouth and this is what we take from it...

The coordinates give no indication of the hardships... What are the terms of it worsening... The whole time running... The decrepit parts are razed... The museum of art is among the first... Hard blows and then dust... The bodies roll into the street... I stumble and it carries on... The whole of it surveyed... Through the pinholes of cameras and finely calibrated instruments... The brown lands are deplored for the sake of this architecture... It is for the monuments that we do this... We stand each on one side or other of the monument and it is the same monument... It is grizzled and unbecoming... With and without posturing... A malady and it is asymptomatic... Still the smell of it abounds... In the streets mistaken and inside as well... A design of disassemblage... Philosophy was cheap even then... We defected across state lines which proved to be defective... The fur wearers smug on the avenues and in the tea parlours... Obscene in their animalia licking the crumbs from table tops... I try to remember something specific... Now... In the time of stopping and starting... It is not memory or a book... It is all so confused now... The painted eyes of a boy in the dark room all at once... Were there microphones there... Or a leaflet... I peeled the clothes back and I was dreaming... First the mouth then the body... It was out of order... The clothes and then the shouting... Nervous... All of us tempting... The hard parts against me... But I was the hard part hardening... She is handed a watershed without rivers... A dry hill and a coma... You push the deaths at me... And several more... For once there is nothing... It is not what is made of it... A thing real... Severances and belittlements... If it were mine I would kill it... Stroke it up and then back... He chokes back liking... Rows of small towns catch fire and the same voice garbles a single catastrophe... It manages... None of which spent on frivolities... You found it first then hit it... A dream of misdirections with feet pointing one way... There was no need for... In the way unsettled... It is your town and you say so... For each one... It turns up in the mannerisms... There is malevolence and you disguise it... This many miles to the dam and you don't believe me... I run out and then in...

It is the same direction... The wall here and here a wall... It is not symmetry but greed... You choose the same thing over again... It might hack away at the indecencies... Curtail the beseeching... I want none of it... Who will feel it first... There is disgust and acrimony... It has a bad taste but the mouth is good and it opens... None of it is permitted and this is as we proceed... I was alone and so arrogant... There were water stains and a pipe with heat running through it... The building bore its own weight... We anticipated... We were not disappointed... The window closed loudly and did not shatter... Nothing broke... It seeped in... Of the remaining bodies only two are recognisable... Remind me again... Were we conscious even then... There were many significances and only one way to approach them... It was burdensome and so necessary... You catch on... I wait and then stumble... The bullet shears an arm and there is dancing... The discordance is in time... Neighbourhoods and they are dismal... The smudges on an art map... Reiterating a disaster... A compression... I paint the eyes shut and listen... It happens that... In a single year the bed and the brother... There is the one who is wistful and the one who declines... I push it out the door... It tears or crumbles... The faceless gods and their brethren... Cocksucking the newborns... It figures the prepuces for the sake of some slaughter... The events have no concordance... With or against time... It dances or it swindles... The music made louder than the machine by the machine that makes it... I must remember you as someone else... Unhindered... An unusual smell... Now that the march is upward... I see it coming... In the dreams then in the faces... In anticipation... I look for it... This is as it accumulates... As an inheritance... A forbidden thing... It seeks me out first... Nominally but still... It is all so far-fetched and I will it nonetheless... As a premonition... Or a terror... You make small accusations and they become big... You say that there is nothing to say and say it again... The way a room conforms or disfigures... A thing turned against the mouth that commits it to language... Open and fine... Not middling nor minuscule... Rains and the people in droves... I see it coming and mind myself... A café in the public way... With walls of its own... And a narrow corridor... Each leads elsewhere and the travail is predicted... Who was wistful... The camera laid eyes on it and they toppled overboard... Windswept or wanton... I run up and you signal to measure the distances... You do this... I run off... Theatrical... We are poised... You at one edge and me opposite... With a boundary marking dusk from the boulevard... The scene as it happens... Tersely calculated gestures... A choreography of moving over... Spatial catastrophes... In the event there is a force and it is diminished... There is the one who desires... The room is vertiginous... We make it over and then some... Tugs of flesh... I go blind and regain my vision... What I see is disgusted... Its entire nakedness... You counsel dispassion... Drive it in and down... I go back to the museum... Through the door and past the cliffs... I lie down in it... Sway to the sound of it... Moaning and derision... The lover dies first... And subsequent... In a feverish torpor... The histories and they are favoured over the others... The scratched out passages... A voice and it is too hoarse to listen... The swollen craters and they erupt one after the other... I touch each of them and heave in secret... In sequence... The turned pages and trauma... Pronounced... As in a dream... With its difficulty... They are pustulant as they present themselves... Each of which overtures... I overtake them... You deride this possibility... Every bit as much as the next one... I throw up undecidedly... The grammars lose their time... It is too much... This accommodation to the niceties... I secrete with them... How else could... You say over an inevitability... The miscreant wanders away... If you had only held otherwise... A play thing in the place of a thing that plays... Inaudibly and unacculturated... It grates on me... Not the discordance... Indeed a harmony and I distrust it... What you pardon is without consequence... I'll have none of it... What your punishments concede... Pronominal impossibilities... The body turned out of an acquired place... Unmarked possessive... I say mine and mingle with the rest... Wounded or hurt it is not the same bird... But it is the same flame ignited by all the public squares... You finish it in one gulp... What you make of this architecture of ransack... I mangle it in your mouth and you bite down hard... Far from conceding... What now and it is over and done with... That it was thought thinking itself thinking... That the newborns divided and choked in the bellies... That the geographies ceased to be surveyed... That the distances were minimal and chided... That the waters rose and didn't stop rising... That we risked the best of what was left and demanded nothing more... Thought nothing of it... The many adorations... They walk each through the door and after... I go after... In the art museum the people are frantic and hungry... They eat the glass as well as the floor... A misnomer in the

place of a thing that is named... It bleeds out...
There is the one who figures and the one who
forbade... The pollutions... Populations in
disarray... What was merciless was not cruelty
but inhibition... The public parks... The
copulations... I got wind of it before you did...
As distasteful as you... We were melancholy
and maladjusted... I undress each one and
make the magnitude of history... It is better
this way and understated... You undress me
first and it goes unnoticed... For centuries the
hermaphrodisms... Even the fictions are
fictions... Contradictions... I kiss it back... It
is cursory and disavowed... The freedoms are
aroused and then settled... At the door... It is
forgone and then forgotten... The columns
collapse first and the people with them... You

come running and it is another body... Infinite and measured... It is never agreed upon... Not the reparations nor the setbacks... The planners measured the distance and it was ruinous... The bodies are sewn into the bodies... Hands to thighs and thumbs to buttocks... Someone laughs first in the great hall or under an umbrella... The philosopher's apology... I push it in deep... The bodies float on a surface of oil or concrete... In the cities especially... City... The named place in which there is walking... The door flies open... Nightly it opens and comes up gasping... I gasp with it and shut it up... It seemed and was swollen... But for forgetting... It was his and then no one's... So I took it... Worn and then wanted... A duffle coat or vibrato... The sexe as it happened... Unfolded... A bathtub and scissor... On the way I drank it down... Fascisms of the order of countries... I could sum it up... The clearance is granted... If I ache in keeping... If the skin catches... The many discrepancies... All of them unnoticed... The sun washes them out... So they say... Small adjustments made for accommodation... For example the building materials... The rents are mismatched with the citizens... For this the wars are immaterial... Numbered and tried... The historiography accounted for it... Touch this part and it is frozen or numb... I cut it out and hand it over... It is the same side and ill equipped for compromise... If it falls... Falters... The conditions are squalid... We sleep and we stiffen... You kiss it in the place where it was… I retch and come running… In the museum of art no one screams or surrenders… Even the bookkeepers raise their heads… The room collides with other rooms… It is a dismal fantasy… I never said… Only dreaded… Still if it happened… It is sceptical and imperfect… Here it is… I set fire to it… In the tall grasses fucking or a floor… It simplifies… Simpers… The small rotting bodies in the woodwork… What limited understanding… We filled full of certainty and decided… Who will swim sinking… Who will or without… There was a wreckage to reckon with… Samples and threatens… The tenants were biopsied and the skins were belaboured… We stand each on one side or other of a skin and we drink it in… If it yearned for some other thing... I was that thing... In the morning unabated... You see through me to it... The thing notwithstanding... Fallen or bereft... I will go then... Still it is rejected... At the outmost point of understanding... Medications and mass burials... The small room is small in comparison to the other rooms... Each fallen in... Who was warned... The boy soldiers all of them... What slackened modernity's decision... My wrath and it accrues... The city is a genocide... Even the philosophers concur... There is a scum on a surface... I peel it back and you cough it up... It is thick and unsightly... A fist raised in aid of what... It is still the same language rotting the interiors... Statistically we were uncompromising... For the same reason... The same humanism... And it was humiliating... Libations and barbary... The horse-drawn miscreants in their carriages... The statements of evidence accumulate... Preachers of imbecility... I'll have none of it... The wire-tap and treachery... The dugout is strewn with forgotten things... Each has a measure that is incalculable... Each and every other... I carry them to the Broad and throw them in... I haul them up to Berry Head and toss them overboard... I speak to them as I would to no person... Sometimes shouting... How could you... How could you... The rest is lost to reason... Fantastical or forlorn I draw it all in... Fold the maps over and trample them... The distances are hysterical... They are preached as such and I for one... In the earth with all the rest... She is wrapped in a sheet and interred... What follows is of the order of an explosion... A series of explosions... Of varying intensities... The countries will not make amends... The strip of desert is bombarded... The sounds enter me through the small animals... And they are sterile... You startle then curse... The sequence may not be predictable... But familiar at the last... Who dreamt of your waking... The shopkeepers were ravenous and indiscreet... It is recorded and misplaced... The pedophiles were as bad as the believers... One atop the other... At the highest point we flooded... Just like the cities... Each thing mistook another thing... I counted them backwards into the water... The disorders were distinct from the rest... Each has an inscription and it is rubbed out... You rub it out and I watch as you do this... It imparts nothing... I grab for it anyway... Suspended... The lanterns are strung across... We refuse them and look elsewhere... Make other decisions... Even if it mattered... The fervor of nihilists... It is for the sake of the liberations that we do this... The temporalities are beguiling... There is always after... We say this and we mean an other thing... Several perhaps... Any other thing... Hope is for martyrs... You hit your fist against it... I grow tired with the centuries and the architecture... Several attempts are made... We run into the ground and are watchful... We count out the differences... Each time fallen... The blood washes out and

then in... I forgive none of it... The mere
mention... It is here in the corner... I put it
there and turn back... Can you blame me...
The shadows cast wishes and fall... I fall with
them... Many mispronouncements are made...
Who do you think... Who looked and who
saw... We all had misgivings and so gave
nothing... What mattered most was history
in the way that things mattered... I step aside
for the cavalcade... At Charonne like at
Mostaganem... Who makes the father dance...
A pardon is granted and rejected... The
fascisms are compelling... I make it this far...
Adverse and objectionable... The versions are
condensed into one version... Its differences
enumerated... If it fell flying... If it damaged
the sun... If the whole of it worried... If stolen

and one... I go down with it... We were asperous even when... And aspired to iniquity... The nations make the exclusions... We speak each on one side or other of a name and it is the same name... I dread them... Each one of them... In the museum the rooms fit each into one another... We are ashamed of them as we enter... We enter and touch the walls... All the buried things arise... The rivers with the bodies of everyone... Each save the first one... It crawls over me... There was one language and this was the son... I refuse the offerings... There are flowers in a vase... I throw them down... We wake and are watchful... The bodies accrue and we name them... Small rashes that spread over the skins... Our languages become enlarged with the grief... The grievances... You yell first and I yell past you... The table breaks into many unrecognisable parts... It is for the familiarity that we do this... That we stand each on one side or other of a death and make the same demands... And they are restless... The story ends repeatedly... In the cities the walls are built with gusto... The painters come later and cover them over... I call out in sleep... The colours become detached... In the middle part the crumbling... Where my fingers claw at the mattress... The man goes to the small house in the country and puts his body inside the sleeper... The sleeper sleeps and is woken... The shutter flickers and catches... There is a catch... That the cry is swallowed by the atmosphere... That the wind tears the roads up... That the dandy is made to close his mouth... At a table the mockeries... At a roadside the spill... I want never to go there... I go there still... What is inevitable is not the war but the language that determines the war... In speaking... I pull at you regardless... You make amends... In the morning you fold the blankets and unwrap the body... I say nothing... The door remains closed and I whisper... Failing that there is the accumulation of sweat... I remark on this... The sweat there and there... It makes rivers out of anger... I remark on this also... It drowns and I follow for a while... What you accuse is the voice that makes accusation... It is for the sound that we do this... That we strangle and bolster... We were incapacitated by our conviction... The statistical improbabilities... For now I say nothing and swallow it down... The house is built again... In the middle of the field... Where the war was won... Where the body fell to the ground... Where the bird flew out... I was the bird... Won for the several unmentioned killings... Won for the punishments... Who pardoned the mother... Who granted the son... There were pleasures to be abandoned... The mouth to begin with... I want the hardest parts and handle them... In the middle ground I stand corrected... If the body flooded with regret... If the name was spoken one more time... If the letter encrypted the flaw... In the other country the people counted out the discriminations... One for each child that was born... One for each mouth and the language that damaged by it... I foresee it and wait until later... It lies down on top of it... You bring me the gravestone... We stand each on one side or the other of the gravestone with hammers and axes... I strike first... We are stricken... We eat with the animals before slaughter... We wipe the blood all over... I beat it back... The hammer breaks and the stone remains solemn... I recognise none of it... The house or the barracks... The country or the slayings... Babbacombe Chelston or Paignton... There is a white house and it is occupied... Where the sentence ends the hotel is made into a confectionery... Teignmouth or Totnes... What the father said was wistful... What the sister retained... None of it is revisited... In the kitchens the blood drains into a bowl... We lap at it... The napkins are old stockings... The beds are river mud... The ceilings are yellowed corsets... The doors are rifle butts... We look past it... We cough it up... You enter and beseech me... In front of the sister you beseech me... I cross the channel at a good clip... I make gestures toward Britanny... You find me anyway... I am lying in the brambles... It lies on top of me... In the city the lights dim early... It makes me visible and untangles what is meant from what is seen... There is an early version and a late version and I am none of these... It mourns with everyone... It cries in the streets... Outside of the houses there is no... You sit at the table and weep... It is for this that I punish you... It is for this that I stay inside the room... It comes and it breaks into pieces... In the inmost component there is a snag and it is attached to a particular memory... I kiss it open... The stench is inviolable... We stand each on one side or other of a pleasure and it is the same pressure... You bring it in and it is incomplete... Incomparable... There is the one who wonders and the one who is pained... I was the predator... You were fortified... The notifications were posted... At the hearing nothing is denied... The one was raving and the other one wept... The minutes dismissed all of it... In movable type... If the executions were applauded... If the weaker ones survived... If the daughter was derided... If the house was occupied... If the bed caught the bug... If you swore up and down... The warning is bestowed... I will go then... It is the same warning... The same war... I attend the funeral in Fallujah and in Hyde Park... Nothing happens and it is written down... There are manifestations... The regional differences are deprecated... I prepare for it clumsily... The groans rise off the moors and out of the hospital beds... The dunes come after... In the sleeping parts... none of which are good enough... We feud like kings and make announcements... How could you... The favours are dispensed... It is cloudy... The body that comes out of the water... It is dead and full of sex... I comb the beach for impurities... I count out the egregiousness... It sucks on me... There are prognoses in languages that are indisputable... Disagreeable... I abhor... It abhors me first... The river floods the undergrounds... Between the thin walls the practices are medieval... It suits you just fine... The technician wanders out... None of it is manageable... The forgetting is indiscriminate... Insistent... What you want... I name each of the vagaries... It startles... You step back... I bring you closer... Into the thick of it... See... It sees past me... You look elsewhere... I grab hold of it... Shake the pieces onto the floor... A rocket launcher in a field of daffodils... The deaths are implanted... Shake shake... Shake shake... Metal particulate and it is bursting... Tiny shards... They are sharp as needles and prick the blood vessels... I anticipate none of it... It goes into the bodies in the strip of land... The radio blasts and we are insensed by it... There is blood that comes out of the ears... The rivers are sucked into the ground... We go underneath to where the passageways narrow... The school collapses from the top floor down... The island slides into the sea and the languages come calling... Over the airwaves... Are there airwaves anymore... I go deaf listening... Lisping... The atrocities are for everyone... We were democratic even then... With finger paint and light fixtures... The doors open and the mirrors come away from the walls... The doors are numbered one to twenty-one... What are you looking at... Does it matter... Matter the masters and their motivations... I won't... Don't... Do it... For now we have the seclusions... We say that we have them and are pleased with the having... Say we for someone... It could be otherwise... You stage the demonstration... We come away from it like paper from a wall... It is limp and poorly attended... What you saw and what you imagined seeing... It was reported and forgotten... In the museum of art the artists are held hostage... It is the same art and it is insupportable... I go there... The moral ground is full of barbs... I trip and stumble... If it were only otherwise... The doors are too narrow... The ships go down with it... I make some progress... You blow on it and it goes out... What lit us up from inside... It was that insidious... We celebrated and died... What came after was impoverished and said to be impervious... You show up... Show me up... I make statistics of it... The beatings the samplings... Would it be preferable... There are seventeen incisions... Four tattoos and five urns two of which are empty... Are you happy with it... What is normal is the deception... The rest is embroidered... One for each of the years... You pull out all the threads and study the stitches... She said beauty was the explanation for everything... The brother the wives... The cistern... We ate it all up... Effluent... Vomitted the rest... Restless... If it died laughing... If it came round... The smallest of tumors... Each one smaller than the rest... You were dispassionate even then... In the room from another century the boy holds out... He holds a body down with one arm and sucks in the rest... There is a sister and bedlam... I kiss it hard... The confusions are arrested... The door there and beyond the door... The carpet absorbs the spill... Twenty-five years between a man and his brother... Between a woman and her son... She drives them back... In the caverns the eyes of the salamanders fall from their orbits... There is moss and a loudspeaker... If it climbed the wall... If it broke out... If it worsened or fainted... If it lied loving... The member is weakened... The digits break off... We are feral... In the hidden parts... Forested and moribund... The orchestra goes round and round... It is no bother... The brother comes to the door and it is epochal... Smuggled in... What comes out of me is acrimony... I walk up again... Who faulted the survivors for surviving... The voices are lifted and carried out... I call up a future... The furniture doesn't arrive... The room is glass or concrete... It is only possible to see in... What the philosopher never said... She banishes the thought... What perished there... If it kissed the ground... If it rotted out... If it choked on me... Throttled... It doesn't leave... The mouth a monstrosity... It presses me... I walk as far as the harbour... I do these things... There are bunkers and an officiant... I see none of it... In the remaining cities the people set fire to themselves... I run in... The ceiling comes down from the rafters... In the rubble there is a firmament and a piece of glass... I stop counting... You kiss me first... It loosens... We do this... It is for the century that we do this... We say that we do this and we do it again... I was unmatched and corrected... The names are confiscated with the effects... The nations are praised with the prisons... I say what needs saying under my breath... In the room there is none of it... And it is affected... Faint scratching under boards... Unpardoned actions... It matters less than you know... The hunters gored the children with the boars... It was accidental... Catastrophal... The mediators were unsuspecting... We spoke once and were silent... In the middle room the shouting was loudest... In the street no one spoke... The body was not a body as I had imagined it...

The sidewalk detached from the wall... Did you hear that... I sit under the window as it shatters... In two years ten thousand bunkers... I make amends with the thief... Seven countries... The gunner is disappointed... I occupy myself with the detriment... It is crucial and congratulated... At the tribunal we are overheard... Six thousand kilometres... There is a riser and we are not included... On the floor... Did you... Were we marred... Martyred... There is a thing that isn't said... Here on the window sill... I crouch against the glass for sufficiency... I do this... They rush at me... Charge through the door or the chimney... The excuses are dusted... Accusations... It is unheard of in the other country...

Facilitated... The voice of the reader mocking ... A teapot and a sewing machine... The fixation on prayer... I spit up... Lie down for a time... There are holes now where there were none...

To Michael O'Leary ... Les personnes qui se parlent se confirment uniques et irremplaçables. ... Jamais coïncidence, toujours proximité. Emmanuel Lévinas

We drank that mud, it ran between our lips; until we felt nothing more of our thirst. We woke, at evening; we could move and walk again. You then used the last of your strength to hit me with your fists, on my face, my chest, blaming me for your thirst, and for having drunk that.

BERNARD-MARIE KOLTÈS

One doesn't die alone, one is killed, by routine, by impossibility, following their inspiration. If all this time I have spoken of murder, sometimes half camouflaged, it's because of that, that way of killing.

DANIELLE COLLOBERT

Architecturally, the text operates a form of confinement, manifest as a continuous block of text from end to end. If one of the active functions of this work is compression, it is the compression not just of a body in a carefully controlled space, but of all the possible spaces pressed into that body, upon which the pressures of historical violence and its attendant catastrophes come to bear. It is this thing which is accountable that detaches from the text, making its own press into the surrounding areas.

Spacially, the room is finite. But what enters, through the body of the speaking voice, orients thought away from its confines toward an exacerbated awareness of endlessly forming breaches. This is no threshold: it is a reiterated collision that belies the possibility of situation. Sisyphus, outdone.

NS

ISBN: 978-0-9844598-0-3

Design and typesetting by HR Hegnauer
Cover concept by John Vincler
Text set in Cochin

Cataloging-in-publication data is available
From the Library of Congress

Distributed by University Press of New England
One Court Street
Lebanon, NH 03766
www.upne.com

Nightboat Books
Callicoon, New York
www.nightboat.org

NIGHTBOAT BOOKS

Nightboat Books, a nonprofit organization, seeks to develop audiences for writers whose work resists convention and transcends boundaries. We publish books rich with poignancy, intelligence, and risk. Please visit our website, www.nightboat.org, to learn about our titles and how you can support our future publications.

The following individuals have supported the publication of this book. We thank them for their generosity and commitment to the mission of Nightboat Books:

Kazim Ali
Suzanne and Nicholas Chapis
Sarah Heller
Elizabeth Motika
Laura Sejen
Benjamin Taylor

In addition, this book has been made possible, in part, by a grant from the New York State Council on the Arts Literature Program.

State of the Arts

NYSCA